This book is dedicated, with my thanks, to Leentje, Keith, Marc, Miss Pickering, Rachel, Jan, Nicki, Marcelle, Simon, Becky, Claire, Jason, Alex, Carl, Matthew and the Spriggs family.

Flower Shops
& friends

A year's journey around
English flower shops

by Sally Page

THE FLOWER SHOP

Published by Fanahan Books

When I am working on a book I always appreciate the help I receive from others,
but this time there were some people I was especially grateful to.
Part-way through researching this book I was struck by an illness that affected my eyesight.
Photography was a struggle. Driving was impossible.
I would like to thank Gillie Strang who drove me to Cambridge and who drank with me there,
my Mum and Dad who took me to Stamford, my daughter Alex who drove me to and from Tisbury
and Martyn and Gay Jose who escorted me to Petworth.
But most of all I would like to thank Billy Kelly who is always there by my side.

Text copyright © Sally Page 2008
Photography copyright © Sally Page 2008
Design & Layout copyright © Billy Kelly 2008
Picture editor: Billy Butler

First published in 2008
Printed and bound in China by C&C Offset Printing

© The Complete Hen by Elizabeth Coatsworth by kind permission of Elizabeth Gartner
© Love Comes Quietly by Robert Creeley by kind permission of Marion Boyars Publishers

Also by Sally Page: The Flower Shop - A Year in the Life of an English Country Flower Shop
and
The Flower Shop Christmas

A CIP catalogue record for this book is available from the British Library

ISBN: 978-0-9553779-2-1

For sales contact:
The Manning Partnership
6 The Old Dairy,
Melcombe Road,
Bath, BA2 3LR.
Telephone 0044 (0) 1225 478444
Fax 0044 (0) 1225 478440
E-mail sales@manning-partnership.co.uk

Distribution: Grantham Book Services

Published by Fanahan Books, Evelyn House, Leddington Way, Gillingham, Dorset, SP8 4FF
www.englishflowershop.com

Those of you who shared with us a year in the life of an English country flower shop,
or who joined us for a warm, cheerfully cluttered Flower Shop Christmas,
will not be surprised to hear me say, I have a passion for flower shops.

In a flower shop you see the seasons come and go as different colours, blooms and fragrances cross your doorstep.
As a florist you are privileged to glimpse every aspect of human life.
You share secrets and sorrows and you watch as people quietly go about helping and thanking each other.

These are the tales a flower shop tells and, as I was to discover, these stories are being retold all over the country.

Introduction

I was beginning to feel like Mole. Something was stirring in the air; things were on the move and I had a growing sense of wishing to go out and about to explore. I loved my work in the village flower shop but I wanted to seek out and discover other flower shops, to hear their stories and their flower shop secrets. I wanted to take to the open road.

This is the story of that journey. Over twelve months I travelled up and down and round about England searching for beautiful flower shops and talented florists.

My journey took me up into the mountains and down to the sea, through country villages and into elegant towns and busy cities.

Each time I returned from a trip I would visit Ted Martin Flowers to tell Ted and Jennifer about what I had found, stopping to lend a hand when they were busy and to share tea and the occasional glass of wine with them. Then, refreshed, I was off again.

So put what you're doing aside – the ironing, the accounts, all those chores you should be attending to can wait – and join me travelling to some of the most beautiful parts of England. Spend some precious time amongst the flowers whilst we eavesdrop on these flower shops' communities.

As we travel we will make many new friends and some old friends will meet up with us along the way. The florists we visit are kind enough to let us share in the lives of their shops and they will introduce us to customers who generously invite us into their homes and businesses.

And as we journey around England we will find time to discover interesting pubs and restaurants, charming places to stay and quiet corners to enjoy some coffee and cake. Now doesn't that sound better than the ironing?

The journey

The Flower Shop
Ambleside

Yarm
Carl Banks

The Green Pavilion
Buxton

Potting Shed Florist
Navenby

Vaas
Nottingham

blue
Shifnal

Miss Pickering
Stamford

Linton
the flower boutique

The Bay Tree Hotel
Burford

Rachel Lilley
Bath

White Gdn
Henley on Thames

Tisbury
Ted Martin Flowers

Spriggs
Petworth

Smith Street
Delicatessen
Dartmouth

January: *Linton, Cambridgeshire.*
February: *Nottingham.*
March: *Stamford, Lincolnshire.*
April: *Bath.*
May: *Shifnal, Shropshire.*
June: *Henley-on-Thames, Oxfordshire.*
July: *Dartmouth, Devon.*
August: *Navenby, Lincolnshire.*
September: *Buxton, Derbyshire.*
October: *Ambleside, Cumbria.*
November: *Yarm, North Yorkshire.*
December: *Petworth, Sussex.*

The Florists' Lunch: *The Bay Tree Hotel, Burford, Oxfordshire.*

January
in Cambridgeshire

the flower boutique

On a pale, chilly day in January I begin my flower shop journey in the village of Linton in Cambridgeshire. The air is sharp and frosty as I walk down the main street towards the village stream and The Dog and Duck pub. On the left, just before the pub, is the flower boutique, the small shop front fresh and bright with early spring flowers.

The first thing owner, Leentje Van den Eede, does when I arrive is to hurry across to the pub to fetch us two hot cappuccinos. The second thing she does, I am glad to say, is to tell me to call her 'Leen', as I am clearly struggling to pronounce her Belgian name. Leen moved to East Anglia with her English husband, Rob, fairly recently but she is proud to say that her shop is now officially one year old.

I gather from Leen that since she settled here she has been made very welcome in the village. Next door is a small shop selling antique jewellery and in the window I can see the owner, eye-glass in place, mending watches. Leen explains that this elderly gentleman often calls in to check on her during the day.

The shop is a mass of flowers the colours of sherbet and sorbet and Leen says how much she enjoys seeing these spring flowers arrive into the markets with the new year. It is a time, she continues, when customers like to treat themselves, brightening up their homes after the Christmas decorations have been put away.

11

Leen prepares 'thank you' bouquets for the mothers of a bride and bridegroom for a forthcoming wedding. As she lines up the roses, lisianthus and anemones, she smiles and says that it is very important that the bouquets are both the same size. Behind Leen on the wall is pinned a picture of another Belgian, Audrey Hepburn, arranging flowers. It strikes me that the two women have the same gentle look about them.

As she works I ask Leen about how she met her husband, Rob. She explains that she had only been in England for three weeks when she and a girlfriend called into a pub for a nightcap on their way home from an evening out. She says Rob walked in with a friend and that, she sighs, was that.

Get Well Soon

Leen's small niece, Eve, is in hospital for an operation on her sinuses so Leen arranges a girly posy in shades of pink for her. It is good to have an aunt who is a florist.

The Best Medicine
Extra blankets on my bed,
Cool plump pillows for my head.
Tucked up tight with all my bears,
Marmite toast cut into squares.
Watching Disney on TV,
Heinz Tomato Soup for tea.
Creep out softly, close the door.
I yet might live past forty-four.

Flower orders are lined up on the brick floor and in the old fireplace ready for delivery. An elegant bouquet from a husband to his wife bears an anniversary message to celebrate ten thousand days of marriage. We get out the calculator and work out that this must mean the couple have been married for just over twenty-seven years.

flower shop secrets
LEEN'S SECRET

Florists always tell customers how important it is to re-cut flowers when they get them home because it takes no time at all for the stems to seal over, making it difficult for the flowers to drink. However, Leen points out that there are certain spring flowers that are exceptions to this rule. The sap of daffodils and narcissi are poisonous to other flowers so she recommends you do not re-cut their stems if you intend to mix them with other varieties.

Flowers for the Stables

At Spain's Hall in the village of Finchingfield preparations are under way for a promotional event which is being held in the newly converted stable block. Leen unloads flower arrangements she is providing for the occasion from the back of her van, which she has parked to the side of the Hall. Parts of the house date back to the fourteenth century and the current owners, the Ruggles-Brise family, have lived here since the 1760s.

Sir Timothy Ruggles-Brise proudly shows us around the stables – and his pride is well justified – the buildings are beautiful. The mellow colours of the old wood and stone are brought to life by the light streaming in at the windows and by the up-lighters that are set into the floors. Sir Timothy says that his only sadness is that the talented architect who designed this wonderful conversion died before he was able to see it completed.

With such a long history Spain's Hall has many stories to tell. My favourite relates to William Kempe who lived here in the 1620s and who, it is said, accused his wife of being unfaithful. On finding out that he was wrong he took a vow of silence for seven years and in each of those years he dug a new pond. I can't help wondering what his wife thought of this.

Tucked snugly into a mirrored cube is a posy of hyacinths, ranunculus, veronica and roses. Leen has used very little foliage in her arrangement and she explains that this is a style that is popular in New York, which is where she trained as a florist.

Leen's first experience with flowers came when she started studying at The Botanical Gardens in New York after which she went on to work as a florist at The Waldorf Astoria Hotel and at The Plaza Florist on Park Avenue. She says that it was at The Waldorf Astoria that she learnt the most – and it seems she had a good teacher there as her mentor, Dieter, had been private florist to the Queen of Belgium.

Leen tells me that they helped decorate some of the amazing parties and weddings held at the Waldorf Astoria including one held by a rock star which the florists were also invited to. I ask about the arrangements that people bought as gifts from the shop and she explains that most bouquets were sent out already in vases and almost all were delivered. Leen laughs, "Nobody carries anything in New York."

Delivering to Cambridge

Cambridge is about ten miles from Linton and the flower boutique's pale turquoise van is often seen wending its way through its labyrinth of streets, as they deliver bouquets and call in to provide flowers for the businesses there.

Leen suggests we visit one of her clients later in the day, a restaurant called Alimentum. We can then take our time to look at the flowers and can also try out their tempting menu. So that evening I find myself very happily ensconced with Leen, talking flowers and life, whilst eating fabulous food and drinking delicious wine. This is exactly the sort of flower shop travel I like.

The next day I decide to explore Cambridge and I wander happily through the colleges and parks, dodging the bicycles as I go. Looking down, as I walk through the centre of the city, I am enchanted to see that the streets of Cambridge are paved with flowers. And propped up against a window I spot a bicycle laden with snowdrop plants. It seems I am not the only one in Cambridge who loves flowers.

*"Oh might I wander there,
Among the flowers, which in the heavenly air
Bloom the year long!"*
Robert Bridges

Walking along by the river I see a group of students and professors heading towards me, gowns flapping behind them in the wind. A passer-by tells me it is Graduation Day in Cambridge and I watch as small bands of students and parents make their way towards the colleges.

On one of my trips to the flower boutique I persuade my friend, Gillie, to join me. She decides escaping for a day or two from the farm, which she runs with her husband, Richard, near Tisbury, is a great idea and we arrange to meet up with Leen in Cambridge. It is easy to spot Leen as she walks across the courtyard of Pembroke College since she is carrying a large bouquet of pink lilies and pale peach roses.

Flowers
for Katie

It is at this point we discover we have a problem. There is a delivery of flowers that has no home as the recipient has gone away. Leen could take the flowers back to her van but this is parked some way away and she would much rather stroll with Gillie and I to a nearby coffee shop. Leen decides the perfect solution is to flag down a passing student and make a present of the bouquet to her. Katie, who we discover is in her third year at Cambridge studying law, is delighted. And so are we.

We chat on through the afternoon and find out more about Leen and her love of flowers. Her business is relatively new but it seems that word about her is spreading and she already has weddings booked for this summer. However, she tells us that one of her favourite weddings so far was booked very much at the last moment. The couple had been forced to postpone their original wedding date as the bridegroom collapsed on his stag night as a result of an undetected brain tumour. Months later when he had recovered the couple decided to get married at short notice and Leen says it was a real pleasure to be able to help them with their flowers.

A florist can never resist flowers and Leen and Gillie investigate the flower stall at Cambridge market.

LEEN'S FAVOURITES

Flower: *White hyacinth.*

Book: *Anything by Paulo Coelho.*

Film: *Nuovo Cinema Paradiso.*

Food: *Fish Pie.*

Drink: *Red wine, especially Montepulciano, as it reminds me of my honeymoon.*

Fragrance: *Black pepper and nutmeg.*

View: *The Suffolk fields in the morning on my way to work.*

Animal: *My cats Louis and Minnie.*

Record: *Come Away With Me by Norah Jones.*

Thank you Leen

February
in Nottingham

It is on a slate-grey February day in Nottingham that I discover the Dutch name for vase is vaas (although both are pronounced the same). And it is in an elegant, high-ceilinged shop of the same name that I find Marc Hagerty and Keith Murphy, the owners of this contemporary but luxuriant flower shop.

Vaas

As soon as I arrive the kettle is switched on and I am welcomed with a cup of very good coffee, in fact, Marc tells me, one bride told him recently that it was because of the quality of their coffee that she picked them to create her wedding flowers. The smell of fresh coffee mingles with the scent of creamy narcissi and I sit back and admire the interior of this interesting building.

Keith explains that they have learnt a lot about the building from some of their customers who knew it before it was a flower shop. One lady told them that she used to change babies where their till is now situated when it was a nursery and another recalled waltzing across the broad, wooden floor during its days as a dance school. Keith has also heard that in the fifties it was Nottingham's first blue cinema but, he laughs and says, that none of their customers have mentioned visiting it then.

Marc & Keith

Both Keith and Marc have come to work with flowers after having had careers in other areas; Keith was a headmaster for many years and Marc worked as an interior designer. Marc's design flair comes to the fore when he is working with brides on their wedding plans and he is able to draw his ideas for them. He also helps to bring his and Keith's ideas to life by producing storyboards which go on to become a memento of the wedding.

Marc's design background is obvious in his approach to buying flowers and he explains how he likes to buy a palette of colours each week for the team to work from. I love this idea and on my numerous visits to the shop I notice that it never looks the same.

A Palette of Flowers

flower shop secrets
MARC'S SECRET

When Marc is considering putting a palette of flowers together he thinks of the flowers as having different personalities, so in the same way as he would not mix certain people together he does not mix certain flowers. For example, he suggests, you would not sit a very robust flower next to a timid flower. He says when he thinks about the flowers in this way it is quite easy to know what mix of personalities he wants around the table with him. This same approach can be used when picking flowers to go in a bouquet or in an arrangement.

Winning Hart's

Situated across the city from Vaas, near to Nottingham Castle, is award-winning restaurant Hart's. Converted from the wing of an old hospital, the building is an attractive mixture of warm, red brick and modern expanses of glass. Vaas has been asked to help prepare the restaurant for Valentine's Day, which is in two days' time.

I help carry in boxes of roses that will be used to decorate the tables, whilst Keith and Marc unload large modern arrangements of anthuriums they have created for the windowsills. I loiter in the restaurant studying tonight's menu, which looks very inviting, even if I don't know what beignets are!

Hart's fixed dinner menu

Pea soup, truffle beignets
Iberico chorizo, capers, wild rocket

Gilthead bream with shellfish tagliatelle
Pork cutlet, bubble & squeak with
caramelised apples, Madeira sauce

Crème Bruleé, raspberry sorbet
Rhubarb crumble, vanilla ice cream

The roses are red, the tables are set and the Champagne is on ice.

flower shop secrets
KEITH'S SECRET

When Keith was asked to prepare a number of bud vases with a single rose in each he thought how much nicer they would look if the roses were cut short so the flowers were level with the top of the vase. This has the added advantage of holding the flower head upright so it is unlikely to droop.

KEITH'S FAVOURITES

Flower: *Snowdrop.*

Book: *Captain Corelli's Mandolin by Louis De Bernieries.*

Film: *The Last Emperor.*

Food: *Prawns.*

Drink: *Vodka.*

Fragrance: *Sea air.*

View: *In Capri looking out over the rocks to the sea.*

Animal: *My old dog, Duncan.*

Record: *Heard It Through The Grapevine by Marvin Gaye.*

MARC'S FAVOURITES

Flower: *Guelder rose.*

Book: *The Five People You Meet In Heaven by Mitch Albom.*

Film: *Dreamgirls.*

Food: *Moussaka.*

Drink: *Vodka.*

Fragrance: *Tuberose.*

View: *The Backs at Cambridge.*

Animal: *My cat Sorrel.*

Record: *And I'm Telling You I'm Not Going by Jennifer Hudson.*

Valentine's Day

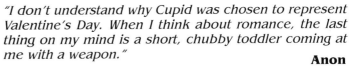

"*I don't understand why Cupid was chosen to represent Valentine's Day. When I think about romance, the last thing on my mind is a short, chubby toddler coming at me with a weapon.*"

Anon

35

Vaas is buzzing with activity, the phones are ringing and the shop looks beautiful. Everybody has been in since the early hours and well over a thousand roses have been unpacked and conditioned. Many are displayed in the shop but there are literally buckets more wrapped and stored behind the scenes. Two of the rose varieties that Marc and Keith have chosen this year are, 'Happy Hour' and 'Bloody Mary' – which I must say rather appeals to me.

The orders are lined up ready for delivery, row upon row, each labelled with the area they are destined for. There are fabulous bouquets, exquisite posies, bottles of champagne, boxes of chocolates and, of course, rich red roses.

Bloody Mary

Happy Hour

37

As I walk amongst the row of deliveries I cannot help taking a sneaky look at some of the romantic messages that are being sent with the flowers. There are many that make me smile and I think it is lovely that people can express their feelings in this way, especially as I know many of the orders will have been taken over the phone.

Keith looks up from his work to tell me about a Valentine order that he took which had the simple message, "I will love you forever". Only, he says, the customer rang up two days later and cancelled it!

A palette of deep reds and bronze, mixed with purples merging into lilac.

"To a beautiful wife and phenomenal mother"

"Truly, madly, deeply"

Stolen Nights

When I visit Nottingham for Valentine's Day my partner, Billy Kelly, accompanies me and we decide that we should steal a little time for ourselves. We stay at Hart's Hotel which is just across the road from their restaurant. It is a modern, stylish hotel with amazing views over an area in Nottingham known as The Park.

The Park is an extensive and fascinating estate of Victorian houses which still has a system of gas street lighting. At night the view from the hotel is a panoramic scene of distant city lights merging with the ghostly glow of neighbouring gas lights.

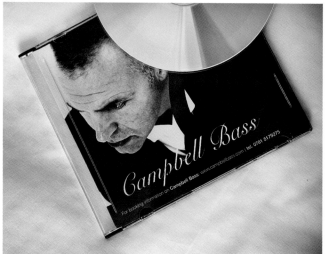

*"I love thee - I love thee,
'Tis all that I can say
It is my vision in the night,
My dreaming in the day."*
Thomas Hood

Reflections

I leave Billy happily drinking beer in the bar and I head up to our room for a long soak in the bath, using all the dreamily scented bubble bath the hotel has provided. There is a CD in the room by a local artist, Cambell Bass, so I listen to him singing old, mellow songs as I wallow in the luxury of these sophisticated surroundings. That evening we meet up with Keith and Marc for cocktails and a thoroughly enjoyable supper. I feel completely spoilt.

Thank you Marc & Keith

March
in Stamford

Pot of hyacinth £25

Miss Pickering
Floral Emporium

Miss Pickering

Travelling through central England on a blustery spring day to visit Miss Pickering's Floral Emporium, I am struck by how engaging the names are of some of the villages I pass; there is Barnwell All Saints, Blatherwycke and Hinton-in-the-Hedges.

Miss Pickering's small and exquisite flower shop is situated in the centre of Stamford and as I walk through the handsome, old stone town towards the shop I recall that someone once told me that Stamford has more churches than any other town in England.

When I meet Miss Pickering I say how much I enjoyed wandering through the streets and she tells me of a bride and groom who have decided to stroll all the way across the town on their way from the church to their reception, rather than being chauffeured by car.

In the window tucked between baskets of daffodils and buckets of hyacinths is a picture of Miss Pickering's shop that has been painted for her by one of her florists, Jo Aldred. Jo, who is originally from Trinidad, tells me that she is a self-taught artist and that she used to run a business painting tile murals when she lived in the West Indies. It occurs to me that everybody has a story to tell and everyone has hidden talents – although I think Jo might be a bit more talented than most of us.

Miss Pickering herself has a number of tales to tell; she started her career as a scientist but then went on to work with Antonio Carluccio importing Italian food. Eventually she turned to floristry working for a well-known London florist before deciding to open her own shop in Stamford, the town where she went to school as a girl.

Jars of Sweets & Ribbons

At the back of Miss Pickering's shop is a small, red dresser on which are displayed old fashioned games, ancient bicycle hooters and jars full of sweets. The names of the sweets take me back to when I was a little girl and I would visit Robin's Corner sweet shop on a Saturday with my dad. There are sherbet fountains, Caramac bars, parma violets and, my favourites, Love Hearts.

On the opposite side of the shop is a narrow, cream dresser and here are stored jars full of ribbons. Miss Pickering pulls a length of pale blue ribbon from a jar to tie a bow around a posy of spring flowers she is making for a teenage girl to give to her friend. Her friend's grandmother has just died and she wants to let her know that she is thinking of her.

Vintage

Since Miss Pickering was a girl she has loved collecting pieces of vintage china. Now such treasures can be discovered on the old washstand and occasional tables around her shop. There are teapots for sale planted with muscari and hyacinths and teacups filled with pretty arrangements of anemones and tulips. Miss Pickering is also known for her 'vintage' bouquets, in which she mixes the soft, faded colours of cottage-garden flowers with aromatic herbs and foliage.

*"Maypole ribbons dancing red and green
In the summer breeze,
Smell of Victoria sponge on the tip of my tongue
And freshly cut grass in the air.
Skipping ropes abandoned on steaming tarmac
And tongues of hair ribbons
That hiss as little girls run."*

Libby Page

The vast sky is a watery blue and the wind is gusting across the fens as Miss Pickering and I drive over to visit Matthew Naylor's daffodil farm. In the farm office there is a picture of three generations of Naylors although, sadly, Matthew's grandfather who started growing daffodils here in 1948 is no longer alive. Miss Pickering and Matthew share a passion for English grown flowers and Mathew tells us of his plans to extend the number of varieties he grows. He has already started to grow delphiniums and peonies.

English Grown

Miss Pickering is here to collect a thousand daffodils (to add to the two thousand she already has in the shop) for a bride who has chosen locally grown flowers for her wedding reception. She says she hopes the guests will be able to take big bunches of them home with them after her wedding. As we talk about the wedding Matthew describes one of his favourite daffodils, called Sarah Markillie, which he named after a friend as a wedding present for her.

Naylor's have been farming daffodils for sixty years and their anniversary recently coincided with the sixtieth birthday of Marie Curie Cancer Care whose symbol is a daffodil. As a result the Naylor family decided to donate sixty thousand daffodil bulbs to the organisation and these were then planted by school children in Hyde Park near to the Fountain of Hope.

flower shop secrets
MISS PICKERING'S SECRET

Miss Pickering suggests that to keep vase water free from the bacteria that can reduce the life of flowers and cause the stems to become slimy and smelly, add half a Steritab or other such water purification tablet to the water with the flowers.

As we walk through the fields Miss Pickering confides that she once thought about marrying a farmer but then, she muses, she thought better of it.

Miss Pickering smiles a little sadly when I ask her about the man she has been seeing recently ... it seems there was an argument at Christmas. As it is Miss Pickering concludes, for the time being at least, she will remain as Miss Pickering.

Miss Pickering
Miss Pickering, Miss Pickering,
Please tell me your name.
Is it Alice or Sophie?
Or Chloe or Jane?

Miss Pickering, Miss Pickering,
Please give me a clue.
Are you Hannah or Flora?
Or Nancy or Sue?

Miss Pickering, Miss Pickering,
Please give me a sign.
I even like 'Gladys',
Just say you'll be mine.

Miss Pickering and her staff create domes of daffodils and pussy willow for a customer who wants to bring a bit of the country into a London meeting in the hope that it will help change the direction of peoples' thinking.

The Olive Branch

The Olive Branch pub and its associated bed and breakfast, The Beech House, are about fifteen minutes from Stamford in the village of Clipsham. It comes highly recommended by Miss Pickering and it confirms one of the things I am beginning to discover on my expeditions – a good florist will often know the best places to eat and drink.

Consequently, when I journey to Lincolnshire to visit Miss Pickering I make a bee-line for The Olive Branch so I can sit by the fire in their atmospheric bar and study their gorgeous menu. The only problem I have is that I want to eat everything on it.

The Beech House Bed & Breakfast

After a relaxing, convivial evening with exceptional food I walk across the road to The Beech House and my welcoming bedroom. I think I would like to end up trying all the different bedrooms at The Beech House but my favourite so far is a room called 'Berry'. Its big antique bed with smooth white sheets and soft pillows stands in a spacious room decorated in warm reds and gentle yellows.

Next door to the bedroom are a dressing room and a restful, stylish, immaculate bathroom that would make any woman happy.

Over breakfast, which is served in a converted barn in The Olive Branch pub, I fall into conversation with the head waiter Antonio. It turns out Antonio, who is from Portugal, is one of Miss Pickering's customers. He tells me that since he has been in England he has become an enthusiastic flower buyer and explains that the English give flowers on many more occasions than they do in Portugal. "Here," he says, "you often see people walking down the street carrying a bunch of flowers under their arm."

Mothers' Day

Mothers' Day is getting close and in the shop everyone is in working hard. Miss Pickering explains that her mother and her sister also pitch in to help and since, on this occasion, my mum has come with me to Stamford it feels like it is a real family affair.

A customer calls in to see an example of the cream tulips that she has chosen for her wedding and asks to buy a big bundle of them. Miss Pickering has to tell her she cannot have them and pretends that they have all been sold, as she knows that her daughter has arranged to send them to her on Mothers' Day. With so many customers coming in to order flowers it is a pleasure to help make up the odd posy or two for the shop. And as the day wears on and florists look like they are flagging I pop into the pub a few doors down and bring back gin and tonics to revive us all. The barman asks me, "Is there a party at Miss Pickering's?" I explain that no, it is just a normal Mothers' Day.

English grown double tulips, looking fat and juicy, are placed in the waiting buckets.

Miss Pickering tries to find space for bouquets that have been boxed up to be collected by the courier.

Florists, Jayne and Jo, are busy working through the orders on the board.

In the afternoon Julie from the nearby Deli calls in with a cake that Miss Pickering ordered for tea.

On Saturday dads start to arrive into the shop with their young children and some of the slightly older children call in with their own pocket money. I watch as Miss Pickering prepares posies and gifts for them. It is amazing what she can do for a handful of coins!

When my mum comes into the shop she is disappointed to see that a vase that she had been admiring has been sold. In fact Miss Pickering has it hidden away so that it can be planted with lily of the valley as a Mothers' Day gift for her.

Next door to the flower shop is a fascinating antiquarian booksellers and the lady from the shop calls in to order some flowers for her mum's grave. Miss Pickering suggests a planted arrangement of spring flowers.

Mothers' Day arrives and it is an early start for Miss Pickering. On her doorstep there is an unexpected caller who has driven up from his home in London to help her out. Christmas argument forgotten, he has come to offer his services as a delivery driver …

Florist Jo with her son Nic

Me and my Mum

With
Buckets
of
Love

Miss Pickering and her Mum

MISS PICKERING'S FAVOURITES

Flower: *Lily of the valley, as it brings back memories of my Grandmother who was called Lillian and wore Yardley lily of the valley fragrance.*

Book: *Agatha Raisin and the Quiche of Death by M.C. Beaton.*

Film: *When Harry Met Sally.*

Food: *Home-made butternut squash ravioli.*

Drink: *Earl Grey tea or Champagne.*

Fragrance: *My cassis scented candle that smells of blackcurrant cane and reminds me of my childhood in Yorkshire.*

View: *The sun setting over Rutland Water whilst walking my dog.*

Animal: *The Hound (also known as Sam).*

Record: *Mona Lisa by Nat King Cole.*

One Last Stop

My friend Sally always says that you can tell the quality of a place by how nice their loos are. I make a mental note to tell her she must call into The George Hotel if she is ever in Stamford. I feel sure she would not only appreciate their excellent food and drink but she would very much approve of their ladies' cloakroom.

The George Hotel commissioned Nottingham artist, Jennifer Bell, to decorate a number of their rooms. I think her paintings in the ladies' cloakroom are inspired – you step into a woodland to be greeted by nymphs scattering flowers and a chubby cherub who is learning how to paint trees.

Driving away from Stamford I dwell on what an enjoyable time I have spent with Miss Pickering and her florists. During my days there her team have always called Miss Pickering by her (very pretty) first name. But, thinking about it I decide, she will always be Miss Pickering to me.

Thank you Miss Pickering

April
in Bath

Rachel Lilley

Walcot Street in Bath is lined with an enticing array of bohemian and quirky shops – you can buy birdcages and mirrors, delicate evening shoes and books that delve into the spiritual and supernatural. It is at the top of Walcot Street, on a glorious spring day, that I find Rachel Lilley's neat and sophisticated flower shop and as I open the door I am reminded of some of the flower shops I have visited in Paris.

At the back of the shop Rachel's assistant, Verity, is busy making up orders; there are flowers for guests staying at nearby Woolley Grange Hotel, arrangements for the King William pub and a 'good luck' bouquet for a customer whose home is to appear this evening on a television programme.

Rachel moved to Bath from London when she decided she wanted a change from her career as a buyer – a career in which she bought everything from handbags to diamonds. It seems her husband Martin also wanted a change and since the move he has pursued his interest in music and Rachel proudly tells me that he has just released his first CD.

Wedding Fair at the Chapel

Rachel fills the small chapel on Walcot Street with samples of wedding flowers so brides-to-be and their mothers can come and see her ideas. There are roses arranged into precise and pretty bouquets, garlanded love-seats and numerous table arrangements.

"What did I know thinking myself able to go alone all the way."
Robert Creeley

flower shop secrets
RACHEL'S SECRET

With their bendy stems and attractive, pliable leaves, tulips are happy to be curved around the inside of a bowl to create a stylish but very easy table centre. It is important to keep an eye on the water level in the bowl as tulips are thirsty flowers and will drain it very quickly.

On a glass stand Rachel arranges a 'cake' of deep red roses beside teacups filled with flowers. It reminds me of our piano teacher's wedding reception which consisted of afternoon tea in a small, icing-coloured temple set in the grounds of an English garden. James, who for years has taught my daughters to play for pleasure rather than for exams, has become a good friend – he is always greeted with a glass of red wine when he arrives for a lesson – and we were delighted when he met and married his lovely wife, Sacha.

"Old clocks chime at half-past-three,
And china roses bloom with tea"
Anon

THE BERTINET KITCHEN BAKERY

Tucked at the end of a Georgian mews, The Bertinet Kitchen Bakery combines a bakery with a cookery school. It is here, in the vaulted room above the kitchens, that Rachel often holds her flower school. The owner, French baker Richard Bertinet, says he loves it when she is here as, "there is flour below and flowers above".

When I join Rachel for one of her classes, mouth-watering baking smells waft up the stairs from the cookery school below.

Today a number of local ladies have joined Rachel to learn how to create hand-tied bouquets. These always look easy to make but I think they are one of the most difficult things to master as a florist. The ladies in the class all do a fantastic job; from Nicky, who is already on a part-time floristry course, to Michelle, who confesses, "I am just hopeless!"

The ladies mix Cool Water roses with magenta hyacinths and purple veronica. Shirley uses the mirror to check that her bouquet is balanced and even.

Rachel tells me that when she teaches floristry to others she feels like she has come a long way from her beginnings as a florist. In those days she would visit Covent Garden market first thing in the morning before going home to experiment making different arrangements with the flowers she had bought there. Rather than waste these early efforts she took them around to the local hospital, some of which, she admits, they enjoyed more than others!

Easter in Bath

Boots & Bunnies

As Rachel opens her shop one morning a gentleman approaches her to ask whether she is the owner. He explains that he has started to pass by her shop every morning to look at her window display as he finds it always cheers him up for the day ahead.

Rachel loves the effect flowers have on people but confides that until recently she found working on funeral flowers terribly upsetting. She says that her attitude changed when a friend asked her to prepare the flowers for her uncle's funeral. After the funeral the friend thanked her and said how the flowers had helped to lift the family's spirits.

The shop is ready for Easter and the window is complete with pink bunnies and vibrant anemones. A customer orders a bouquet to celebrate the arrival of twin boys and Rachel pops two dark purply-blue anemones in amongst a large posy of white flowers.

Verity balances pink Wellington boots on the counter and fills them with branches of cherry blossom. These are going to form the window display of a nearby clothes shop, Toast. The girls in the shop say they always look forward to seeing what flowers they will receive from Rachel each week.

Tulipomania

Dyrham Park is a Baroque mansion nestling in attractive, undulating parkland about ten minutes north of Bath. Every year this National Trust property hosts an event, Tulipomania, in which the beautiful house and chapel are filled with thousand of tulips.

The National Trust has invited their volunteers and church flower ladies to take part in the event, along with flower groups from Chipping Sodbury, Bath and Bradford on Avon. Rachel and florists, Katy Arnold and Christine Priddis, are also enthusiastic contributors.

As I make my way down the steep drive to the house I can see Rachel and Verity unloading vases and tulips from Rachel's Mini. I park my Mini alongside hers (I have a ridiculous thought that they might like to chat) and watch as they begin to arrange the flowers. Behind them in the distance a group of children are playing; some endlessly rolling down the hill and others building a den from fallen branches.

The house, which is closed to the public today, is a hive of activity. In each of the rooms the flower ladies are snipping and arranging, some are quietly concentrating whilst in other rooms there is the sound of chatter and laughter. I cannot think of a nicer way to spend an afternoon than to be allowed to wander freely through this charming house watching the progress.

One of the rooms that Rachel is decorating is the Queen Anne bedroom and she fills the stone fireplace with black and citrus-coloured tulips. I recall that it is because of Tulipomania that I discovered Rachel Lilley, I so admired her arrangements last year that I managed to track her down with the help of the National Trust.

In the Victorian kitchen there is a display showing all the tulip varieties that are being used for the event, although in a bucket in one of the bedrooms I do spot one I have not seen there – a lone hybrid that seems to be a glorious twist of nature. A single white and green tulip that looks as if it has been kissed with pink lipstick.

Flower group member, Jan Jones, adds a finishing touch

Everywhere you look there are tulips. Jackie, the manager of the shop and plant centre, has rows of cerise and black tulip plants ready and waiting for visitors.

At home I still have a mug painted with tulips that I bought from Jackie last year when I visited Tulipomania for a book signing. I always like signings at the National Trust because the ladies there make you so welcome and ensure you are always supplied with tea and cakes.

In the old dairy milky white tulips look perfect against the blue and white tiles and the rows of terracotta bowls.

RACHEL'S FAVOURITES

Flower: *White French tulips*

Book: *A tough one; I read so much. One that really stands out though is Lovely Bones by Alice Sebold.*

Film: *Pulp Fiction*

Food: *Veggie sausage, mustard mash and onion gravy!!*

Drink: *Hot chocolate.*

Fragrance: *Fresh air!*

View: *Sunset over the sea.*

Animal: *Monkey.*

Record: *Another difficult one. I would have to say Primal Scream's Get Your Rocks Off.*

Rachel has also been asked to decorate The Orangery. Arranging antique birdcages and twisted branches Verity creates a fitting display using bowls of plump orange tulips.

As I leave Dyrham Park, after a thoroughly enjoyable day I find that Rachel has left me a gift of long stemmed French tulips on the bonnet of my car. Or maybe it was a gift from her Mini …

Thank you Rachel

May

in Shropshire

blue

In the Shropshire railway town of Shifnal, Jan Park runs her flower shop, blue. On a rainy day in May it is a delight to step inside and wander amongst the banks of early summer flowers. The shop stretches back into a number of interconnecting rooms from where Jan also sells gifts and cards. Up the narrow staircase there is more to explore in the low-ceilinged passages and rooms.

A local department store has called and ordered "garden party flowers". Jan explains that the flower displays will help promote the launch of a new perfume. Jan also sells fragrances and the air in her shop is scented with the smell of fresh flowers and the soft grassy aroma of 'After the Rain' perfume.

An order is taken from a gentleman for his sixtieth wedding anniversary. He tells the girls in the shop that he is proud and thrilled to have been married for so long. A younger man calls in and buys one of the hand-tied posies that are ready and waiting in the metal buckets at the front of the shop. He appears relieved that he isn't going to be asked to choose which flowers he would like!

flower shop secrets
JAN'S SECRET

Jan is a great believer in treating flowers well. The way she conditions gerberas is a good example of this. When the gerberas arrive from market she cuts the stems and making sure their heads are supported she lets them have a good drink. This could be for up to twelve hours. As the stems are upright and they are not taking the weight of the flower-heads this enables them to become firm and strong.

A Studio in the Woods

Jan studied as an artist and it is through her art that she came to open a flower shop. Jan wanted to buy beautiful flowers to paint but could not find a local shop to supply them. When her husband went on business to Holland Jan travelled with him and she saw what wonderful flowers were available from the flower shops and flower stalls in Amsterdam. She decided that as she could not find such gorgeous flowers locally she would start her own shop.

Jan still continues with her art, painting in her studio overlooking the woods near their home. She says it is where she is happiest. Her paintings and textile art are on sale in her shop, the clear colours complimenting the fresh tones of the flowers.

The walls of Jan's studio and home are hung with her art, including projects inspired by family holidays. On one wall rows of driftwood and shell sculptures are displayed, reminiscent of a long walk on a deserted Scottish beach.

Looking around Jan's studio I am drawn to a painting in which the sky is almost black – a stormy and striking mix of navy and purple. It reminds me of the skies you see in Ireland and of another painting I once saw. I did not buy that painting but I still remember it vividly. They always say it is the things you do not do that you regret the most.

Beginning Again

Damp, we swept in from the Dingle street,
Door closed to drown the drum of passing feet.
Between the pencil pots and the painted clouds
I was rooted in thin air.
No history, no anecdotes to smile at and compare.

Climbing up the spiral stair, it came in sight and just in reach,
Plum black clouds sweeping an Irish beach.
Distant green, cool like the draught before the storm.
But we could not afford this beach,
So we left it behind. Just out of reach.

Now we have history. I am rooted to you in air
And breath and flesh and stone.
Yet I still wish our beach was hung in our home.

JAN'S FAVOURITES

Flower: *Ranunculus.*
Also know as Turban Buttercups.

Book: *Always the one I am reading at the moment.*

Film: *Anything by Merchant Ivory; for the era, the settings, the music and the costumes.*

Food: *Anything by Cranks.*

Drink: *Tea, proper tea, not bags, preferably Kenyan.*

Fragrance: *A walk in the woods after the rain.*

View: *The view from my bed over Shropshire countryside. I can see for miles and it is never the same, always uplifting.*

Animal: *Lambs. Their arrival coincides with spring and daffodils and their frolics make me smile!*

Record: *Gloria Gaynor, I Am What I Am… because I am.*

A grandmother comes into the shop desperately looking for a teddy bear as her granddaughter has lost hers and is distraught. The lady had rung the shop earlier and Sara, the manageress, has a soft, sympathetic teddy put aside for her.

A bouquet is being prepared for a new mother who has just had a baby girl.

Sara collects roses ready for a bouquet. She tells me one of her favourite messages that was delivered with roses recently, said simply, "You win."

Looking around her shop Jan recounts how they have been asked by a film company if they could use her shop as a film set. The film is to be about a dancer and the director wants to film one of the characters buying her flowers.

Fat and fragrant English roses are displayed in an old enamel tea pot. These roses were grown by David Austin whose beautiful rose gardens are situated nearby. Jan recalls how they were the first to use the rose varieties David had especially bred for florists. His daughter Claire was getting married and Jan was asked to create her wedding bouquet. I enquire whether Claire liked the bouquet. "She shrieked," she smiles.

Visiting David Austin Roses

About ten minutes down the road from Shifnal are the gardens of David Austin Roses. David Austin started his working life on the family farm in Shropshire but inspired by a book about old roses he decided to become a nurseryman. In 1961 he produced his first rose, which he named 'Constance Spry'. His second rose, 'Chianti', was launched in 1967. It occurs to me that someone who loves old English roses and names them after florists and red wine has to be a thoroughly good man. David Austin Roses remains a family firm with David's son, also called David, working alongside him.

During one of my first summers working for Ted Martin Flowers in Wiltshire, Ted ordered 'Juliet' and 'Emily' roses from David Austin Roses for a bride who wanted fragrant English roses in her bouquet. I realised that the David Austin name was vaguely familiar to me and when the roses arrived I suddenly remembered my Dad pouring over David Austin garden rose catalogues. Other names came back to me, Harry Wheatcroft, Peter Beales and Harkness. All of whose catalogues made enjoyable winter reading for my father.

I visit David Austin's rose gardens with my friend Gay. Gay has three daughters – all of whom, like their mother, love roses. Gay feels these roses are perfect flowers for English weddings and her daughters' wedding photographs, which hang at the top of their stairs, are a testament to this.

Neither Gay nor I have been to the gardens before and we spend a wonderful few hours dawdling from garden to garden admiring the over seven hundred rose varieties that grow there. As I love the name so much, I cannot resist buying a pink fragrant climbing rose called 'The Generous Gardener'.

You Love the Roses

You love the roses – so do I. I wish
The sky would rain down roses, as they rain
From the shaken bush. Why will it not?
Then all the valley would be pink and white
And soft to tread on. They would fall as light
As feathers, smelling sweet: and it would be
Like sleeping and yet waking, all at once.

George Eliot

Gay buys a pink damask-like rose called 'Princess Alexandra' for her daughter Claire. Claire and her husband are desperately trying to sell their house in the north of England to move closer to the family. Claire has just recovered from cancer and with a new job and hopefully soon a new home, Gay wants the rose to celebrate a fresh start for the couple.

A Day of Wine and Roses

After strolling through the gardens we stop for something to eat. In the plant centre there is a cosy coffee shop, but as the weather is fine we decide to sit outside and watch the bustle of the garden whilst enjoying a glass of rosé wine.

"They are not long, the days of wine and roses:
Out of a misty dream
Our path emerges for a while, then closes
Within a dream."

Ernest Dowson

We are both tempted by the home-made cakes which are named after the roses. Rose petals are scattered on the plates and on the earthenware tiles of the counter.

Munstead Wood
A moist country hazelnut cake

Claire Austin
A light zesty, lemon sponge

Skylark
Traditional fruit scone with fresh cream and strawberries

Princess Alexandra
Raspberry, rose petal and ricotta cheesecake

David Austin at Chelsea

After my visit to the gardens David Austin Roses are kind enough to invite me to join them at the Chelsea Flower Show. I have been to Chelsea a few times before, but on this occasion I am allowed to go along on the preview day, which is a real treat for me.

The Fetzner winery garden

It is possible to get a close and lingering look at all the gardens and I even get a glass or two of Champagne as well.

As you approach the David Austin rose garden a heady fragrance welcomes you.

Wake up and smell the roses

Thank you Jan

June
in Henley on Thames

White Gdn

Walking up the street from the river on a bright June day it turns out that all the people I meet and ask directions from know Nicki Barley. Nicki is the youngest of the florists I am to visit on my year's journey and it seems that everyone has a good word to say for her and how hard she works.

Situated on the main street in Henley, White Gdn is a tiny shop but it is bursting with colour and character. Nicki first started working here as a Saturday girl and after studying floristry at college and working her way up, she eventually ended up buying the business from the owners.

It is obviously a busy shop and Nicki is helped by the young college girls she now employs. They tell me of the many deliveries they send and of some of the funny messages they are asked to write. One customer always addresses his messages to "Her Majesty", whilst one signs off, "From the skeleton in the closet".

However, perhaps Nicki's favourite message is, "I may be twenty five years too late and we are 12,000 miles apart but you still make me smile."

Three men in a boat

There are flowers to be organised for summer parties and weddings. A birthday party with a Welsh theme is to be based around green, red and white flowers and Nicki decides to add some leeks to the arrangements as a finishing touch.

Meanwhile, bundles of flowers are carried down to the river and loaded into a boat. A wedding is to take place on nearby Temple Island and this is the only way to get the flowers to the venue. This small island marks the start of the Henley Royal Regatta course and its temple, built in the 1770s, has picturesque views across the water meadows.

Up in the work-room above the shop the kettle is on ready for coffee. I notice that three of the spotty coffee cups have been borrowed to stand broken peonies in. I think they look rather pretty this way.

Henley has been hosting its famous regatta since 1839. The women's event is held at the end of June, with the Royal Regatta in early July.

The town fills with smartly dressed guests and from the doorstep of Nicki's shop I watch a parade of splendid hats and striped blazers file down the street to the riverbank.

As the weather has been unpredictable some ladies have co-ordinated their dresses with matching Wellington boots.

A few years ago some retired rowers, who come to Henley every season, decided to stage a buttonhole competition. This is now a fiercely competitive event and Nicki is asked to make up some of the entries. There are awards for the best buttonhole, the best home-made buttonhole and there is even an award for the worst buttonhole.

"...the pleasant chat goes round in musical under-
tone; while, in the pauses of our talk, the river,
playing around the boat, prattles strange old tales
and secrets, sings low the old child's song that it
has sung so many thousand years ..."

Jerome K. Jerome

NICKI'S FAVOURITES

Flower: *Dahlia ...in pink.*

Book: *Don't sit still long enough to read!*

Film: *Baz Luhrmann's Romeo and Juliet.*

Food: *Italian, with loads of garlic.*

Drink: *My favourite cocktail – Passion Punch.*

Fragrance: *Vanilla or sweet peas.*

View: *When driving home into Henley the view over Henley Bridge down the river. I know I am home and I remember what a lovely place it is to live.*

Animal: *My cats, Meg and Mia.*

Record: *Don't Look Any Further by Dennis Edwards and Siedah Garrett.*

Summer
Living

In the village of Aston, just across the river from Henley, a Summer Living fair is being held. It is taking place in the red-brick barn galleries and extensive gardens of Middle Culham Farm. As I arrive exhibitors are unloading goods and stands from the backs of cars and horse-boxes. It is early in the morning and the most beautiful, clear June day.

An elderly gentleman fills the lawn in front of a barn with pots of magnificent delphinium and iris. To his right two ladies set up another stall displaying a huge variety of home-grown plants. I particularly like the wispy, mauve Japanese anemones that I spot nestled amongst pots of lilac campanula.

The stands displaying crafts and accessories create tempting splashes of colour against the terracotta of the barns and the shady greens of the gardens.

Nicki has a stand in a courtyard overlooking one of the gardens. She has chosen a black and white theme with accents of lime-green. There are hessian bags filled with marguerites and gardenias, chincherinchees mixed with plump peonies, and shiny green apples tucked in amongst mini-gerberas. On a wooden crate she has a tray of cacti in aluminium pots – around the base of each plant she has scattered seeds or pistachio nuts. "The only trouble," Nicki laughs, "is that the chickens have been coming over and eating them."

flower shop secrets
NICKI'S SECRET

When working with woody stemmed flowers, such as hydrangeas, Nicki cuts the stems into a 'V' shape at the base (rather than the slanting cut we would normally suggest). This gives a greater surface area for the water to be drawn up the stem and helps pierce the Oasis if you are using the flowers in an arrangement.

And Oh, the Shoes

In the main barn I come across a company called Floyd Shoes. They sell real 'Doris Day' shoes and I cannot resist trying some on.

My Favourite Things

Kitten heel sling-back with handbag that matches,
Small 'diamond' detail that sparkles and flashes.
Jimmy Choo packages tied up with string,
These are a few of my favourite things.

Toes in silk satin with pink floral beading,
Suede boots and red pumps I really was needing.
Peep-toes that step out when it turns to spring,
These are a few of my favourite things.

Grey smoky court-shoe with teal coloured edges,
Black killer heels and ridiculous wedges.
Crepe-de-chine sandals with soft ribbon strings,
These are a few of my favourite things.

When my shoe bites, when the bill stings,
When I'm feeling sad,
I simply remember my favourite things,
And then I don't feel so bad.

When Nicki eventually finishes work she visits her boyfriend, Chris, at his Tapas bar, La Campana. Chris has just bought the business from his father and the couple are busy putting their stamp on it. The only real problem they have encountered so far is that the low ceiling is not really ideal for Chris (who used to play basketball for England) and he recently knocked himself out on one of the wooden beams.

Chris and his team pride themselves on the quality of their cocktails and to help him practise Nicki agrees to supply flowers for the bar in return for being able to act as a taster. Later in the evening, when the bar is buzzing with good-natured chat, I join them and volunteer my services too.

Mine's a Rum Daisy

Black Orchid: *Pernod, Cointreau, blackberry brandy, tonic, lemonade.*
Rum Daisy: *white rum, lime juice, grenadine, twists of lime and orange.*
Forget-me-not: *schnapps, cherry brandy, kirsch.*
Gardenia: *gin, pineapple juice, double cream, grenadine.*
Mimosa: *Champagne, orange juice.*
Orange Blossom: *gin, orange juice, caster sugar.*
Purple Cactus: *golden tequila, sweet sherry, passion fruit juice, grenadine.*
Rose Cocktail: *dry vermouth, kirsch, grenadine.*

Thank you Nicki

GONE SAILING

July
in Dartmouth

Smith Street Deli

I decide to take the slower, gentler route into Dartmouth, choosing the road that dips down to meet the estuary ferry. As I wait for the ferry I watch the old steam train pass as it chugs across the road and out onto the track to my left, hugging the Devon coastline. Beyond the railway crossing and estuary I can see the pastel coloured houses of Dartmouth and, in the distance on the hill behind the town, the clock tower of the Royal Naval College.

The delicatessen in Smith Street is run by husband and wife, Simon and Marcelle, and combines a wonderful mixture of fine food and flowers. Another important member of the team is their border terrier, Bertie. Marcelle organises the floristry side of the business, Simon the food, whilst Bertie just looks forward to seeing the many customers who make a point of calling in to visit him.

On a cool day in early July the shop is ablaze with yellow sunflowers and purple alliums. In the shop window Marcelle has placed a tall vase of pale blue delphiniums and hot-pink gerberas, into the bottom half of the glass vase she has put handfuls of seashells.

Marcelle and Simon decided to move to Devon after a weekend visiting their friend Simon Hart, who is a local artist. As they walked by the water's edge and through the maze of narrow streets they found themselves falling in love with Dartmouth.

Falling in love with Dartmouth

I visit the gallery that Simon Hart used to own and have a pleasant time imagining all the pictures and sculptures I would buy if I had a bigger house. Sarah, who now owns the gallery, tells me about some of the local artists who exhibit there. In the end I buy a print by Simon Hart so I will have a reminder of my time in Dartmouth. I think I am falling in love too.

Devon Wedding
They married in the church by the sea,
Freesias scenting the salty air.
Estuary and sky stretched smooth as a sheet,
Backdrop to the bobbing hats and sailing silk.
In the distance, splashes of red and white boats
And tidemark boys crabbing, jumpers in a line.

The life of this seaside town keeps Marcelle busy as she supplies fresh flowers to local businesses. Her weekly contracts include flowers for restaurants, pubs, hairdressers and a lingerie shop. I gather from Marcelle that quite a bit of bartering goes on between the businesses.

Being by the sea there are orders to be prepared for weddings that take place on board boats and at the nearby naval college. Flower arrangements are also delivered by water taxi to a floating restaurant moored in the middle of the River Dart.

After a long day in the shop Simon and Marcelle gratefully close the door and walk up the street to their local, The Cherub Inn. The inn is the oldest building in Dartmouth. It narrowly escaped destruction by fire that swept through the street in 1864 and by the bombs that fell nearby during the Second World War. The cherub, which hangs like a figurehead from the wooden beams at the corner of the building, appears to have been watching over them.

There are so many good places to eat and drink in Dartmouth and I do my best to try as many as I can during my visits. I have a memorable supper at the Anzac Street Bistro which is owned by Simon and Marcelle's friend, Serin. I had not heard the name Serin before and Marcelle explains that all the brothers in the family have been named after birds.

One recommendation I particularly enjoy is Taylor's Restaurant which overlooks the inner harbour of the town. As I am shown to a table a gentleman arrives to be greeted by the staff like an old friend. It appears that he comes here every year to celebrate his birthday. He orders a glass of Champagne and sits at a table by the open window admiring the view.

Back in the shop Marcelle is preparing bouquets for delivery. One customer has ordered antique-pink Illusion roses for his wife who is just about to give birth to their first child. He has remembered that she chose these roses for her wedding bouquet. Marcelle recalls another customer who also re-orders his wife's wedding roses. It does not matter where the couple are staying, Marcelle knows she will be asked to make a delivery of Black Bacarra roses to his wife on their wedding anniversary.

But it seems not all men are so romantic. Marcelle remembers a gentleman who always sent peonies to his girlfriend while they were courting – so much so that he was known in the shop as Peony Man. However, once they were married he never ordered her peonies from them again.

Before Marcelle started her flower business she sold fabrics for an interior design company. Looking around her shop it is clear that she has a good eye for colour and shape. A small window display of cheerfully clashing orange and pink gerberas particularly appeals to me.

Marcelle tells me she has her mother to thank for much of her understanding of flowers. She explains that her mother is an experienced gardener and her enthusiasm has been infectious.

flower shop secrets
MARCELLE'S SECRET

Crystallised rose petals are pretty, edible and decorative. They can also be added to Champagne, rather than a sugar cube, when making a Champagne cocktail. Use roses that have not been sprayed with any pesticides, wash the petals and remove the white bit at the base (this has a bitter taste). Dissolve a quarter of a tablespoon of gum arabic in a tablespoon of water and brush this on the petals. Sprinkle the petals with caster sugar and leave on baking paper to dry.

Fine Food & Flowers

Simon originally trained in land management but when his father became ill he gave up his job and moved home to help run the family bacon business. His father recovered and eventually the business was sold. Simon decided that he could now develop his great interest in food by opening the deli in Dartmouth. Luckily, living here he is also able to pursue his other great love by playing rugby for Dartmouth.

Summer Picnics

We hid all summer
In the dunes,
Marram grass
Woven into wicker.
Basket spilling
Tempting parcels
Of inappropriate food.
Pristine plates,
Half-buried islands
At our feet.

We were two
Untidy starfish
In the sand,
Gazing up at
Intoxicating skies.
Bucket and spade
Seaside sounds
Washed up
Into the clouds
Floating overhead.

Digging in
Gritty toes,
We were sheltered,
Hidden,
Warm in our hollow.
Time was drifting,
Shifting sands
Suspended,
Your fingers
Touching mine.

Simon buys as much local produce as possible, including chilli jams and pickles from the neighbouring South Devon Chilli Farm.

When I finally leave the shop I am loaded down with Parma ham, salamis, olives and cheeses. Simon explains that one of the cheeses, Cornish Yarg, only got its name because the makers, the Gray family, could not think what to call it and decided to use their surname spelt backwards.

MARCELLE'S FAVOURITES

Flower: *Stock.*

Book: *The Kite Runner by Khaled Hosseini.*

Film: *Pretty Woman.*

Food: *Spaghetti Bolognaise.*

Drink: *Gin & Tonic.*

Fragrance: *Freesias.*

View: *From the top of the hill overlooking Dartmouth.*

Animal: *My border terrier, Bertie.*

Record: *Lovely Day by Bill Withers.*

Bertie & Alfie

As I walk around the streets of Dartmouth I encounter a border terrier emerging from a pretty black and white house. I am sure this is Bertie and wonder what he is doing so far from the shop. When I call his name Bertie ignores me; he is much more intent on watching a cat poised on the steps below him.

When I get back to the shop Bertie is there to welcome me and it seems that we have a case of mistaken identity. It turns out that I have just met Bertie's friend, Alfie. Marcelle explains that these two are great mates and often like to go out for walks together.

The House on the Hill

Customers Nicky and Simon Marson own what must be the tallest and thinnest house in Dartmouth. It is situated at the top of the town looking out over clusters of roof tops to the sea. When the family is not using the house it is let to guests and the Smith Street Delicatessen is often asked to provide wine and flowers for them.

On a sparkling afternoon in July my daughter, Alex, and I climb up the steep steps to the house to deliver a bouquet and a bottle of wine from Marcelle and Simon.

The ornate wooden carving on the outside of the house reflects the great age of the building but the inside of the house has been transformed by Simon, who is an architect, into a modern, airy home.

Every bit of space is used, including the eves, where a spiral stair leads to a small sitting area and a second bathroom. The white curved beams and bright skylights remind me of being on a boat.

"We built a ship upon the stairs
All made of the back-bedroom chairs,"
Robert Louis Stevenson

Thank you Marcelle

August
in Lincolnshire

Potting Shed Florist

On a warm, sleepy day in August in the village of Leadenham I discover the Potting Shed Florist. Or it might be more correct to say Becky Macnab, the Potting Shed Florist, found me. I met Becky at a flower show earlier in the year and she talked about her business with such love and enthusiasm that I felt it was a shop I had to visit on my journey.

Tucked into the potting shed of an old stone rectory the shop is overflowing with summer flowers, terracotta pots, plants, watering cans and even milk churns. As I settle down for coffee with Becky and her assistant, Jane, I know it has been well worth the trip.

In the corner of the shop there is a pretty arrangement of spray roses and snowberries, which has been ordered by a group of friends gathering for a celebratory lunch.

A woman calls in to send flowers to thank her friend for staying on the phone all night offering words of encouragement and advice as the customer's dog was having puppies. Other 'thank you' bouquets go out to local teachers for the school year that has just ended.

Customers passing through the small courtyard at the back of the rectory into the Potting Shed are often delightfully surprised by the abundance of flowers they find hidden there. Becky perfectly understands their enjoyment and she tells me she feels the same pleasure every time she opens up the shop in the morning.

However, a customer she once shared her fervour with did, she says, look at her quite strangely. He said she would be better off talking to his wife. "Does she love flowers too?", Becky asked. "No", he replied, "she's a psychiatrist."

Undaunted, Becky continues to approach her floristry with genuine ardour. An army officer phones to order flowers for his wife's fortieth birthday. He will be away on her birthday and will not be home until Christmas. I gather from Becky that he wants the flowers to create a real 'wow!' I have a feeling that Becky will know just what to do.

BECKY'S FAVOURITES

Flower: *Blue hydrangea.*

Book: *The Flower Shop by Sally Page.*

Film: *Bridget Jones.*

Food: *Strawberries or raspberries and cream.*

Drink: *Chilled white wine.*

Fragrance: *The smell of the flowers when I open my shop door in the morning.*

View: *My two little girls asleep when I tuck them in at night.*

Animal: *My lovely (and very old and smelly!) spaniel, Hoby.*

Record: *Always & Forever by Heatwave.*

Staying in Stragglethorpe

Becky directs me to Brant House, a charming bed and breakfast in the nearby village of Stragglethorpe. As I pull up outside the house the evening sun is just going down over the garden and the owners, Ian and Catherine, come out to welcome me. I especially like Ian's idea of a welcome as he suggests I get settled and then come down and share some wine with them.

We sit looking out over the garden and I discover that Catherine knows John Bickersteth who is a friend and customer of Ted Martin Flowers. It transpires that John, the former Bishop of Bath and Wells, is a family friend and that he conducted her daughter's wedding service.

As the sun sinks we chat on and Catherine and Ian invite me to share supper with them in their large, friendly kitchen. It is a lovely end to a long summer's day.

"Is not old wine wholesomest, old pippins toothsomest,
Old wood burns brightest, old linen wash whitest?
Old soldiers, sweetheart, are surest and old lovers soundest."
John Webster

In my room crisp, white linen pillowcases rest against the warm and ageing, carved bed head. On the dressing table is a garden posy of roses, sweet peas and lavender.

Burghley

A national magazine invites Becky to provide flowers for their stand at Burghley Horse Trials. Weaving her car between the riders and the horseboxes we draw up near the designated marquee and start to unload armfuls of scabious, rosemary, roses and bluperum.

We fill pastel coloured, enamel jugs and buckets with informal, country bunches.

When we return the remaining flowers to the car Becky shows me a wooden sign she has just collected for her daughters to help them decorate their 'Bunny Cottage'. The cottage was lovingly built by the girls' grandfather who, sadly, died last year. Even though they have outgrown this Wendy house they do not want it dismantled as it reminds them of him. So the bunnies have moved in instead. Becky's husband, Andy, does query whether the rabbits really need floral curtains – but as Becky says, "If they are going to be part of this family they have to learn to respect Cath Kidston!"

The Wedding Morning

The Potting Shed has been asked to prepare flowers for a wedding that is taking place in a country house hotel nestled in the Vale of Belvoir. Langar Hall is a beautiful family home which over the years has gently evolved into a hotel. It is to be a small and very personal wedding and the setting seems perfect for it.

On the morning of the wedding I help to deliver the white rose buttonholes that have been ordered for the guests. These are placed in each of the bedrooms ready for the friends and family who will soon be arriving.

Becky prepares an arrangement of Avalanche roses, thistles and veronica for the room where the ceremony will take place.

The wedding bouquet is carefully wrapped in tissue and cellophane beside a delicate, embroidered heart that Becky makes for each of her brides as a souvenir of the day.

Becky is an incurable romantic and it is obvious that she loves weddings – no matter how large or small they are. She tells me of one wedding where friends and family were asked over to a couple's house for a summer barbeque. As the guests arrived they were led through the field at the back of the garden to the church where the vicar was waiting. The bride carried a very simple bouquet and all the congregation wore shorts.

Individual cakes, one for each of the guests, are arranged in tiers and decorated with roses. By each place is a name card tied with raffia to a small bunch of flowers.

As a finishing touch a heart wreath is tied to the door to welcome the bride and groom.

flower shop secrets
BECKY'S SECRET

Why only have a wreath on your door at Christmas time? Becky believes first impressions count, so when friends are visiting she likes to have something to welcome them. She hangs a twig heart wreath on her front door all year round and then adds seasonal things to the basic wreath as the seasons change, such as fresh lavender from the garden or berries and fruit in the autumn.

Moving on

The time comes when the business outgrows the potting shed and the shop moves to bigger premises in the village of Navenby. It is not a decision that Becky takes lightly as it involves buying the new shop. Becky admits that she and Andy are by nature cautious, not even using a credit card. She explains that they did keep one for emergencies but to ensure they were not tempted to use it very often they hid it in the garage, in the freezer, in a tub of ice cream!

Within the first week the couple are reassured that they have made the right decision. On their open weekend the shop is heaving with over six hundred customers. Andy looks distinguished in a dinner jacket as he serves Bucks Fizz and flower-shaped shortbread. As one customer glances at the chandeliers, Becky overhears her say, "It's lovely, it's a posh potting shed."

159

One guest they are particularly pleased to see is Pat who is godmother to Andy and their daughter Emily. Pat is the sort of fairy godmother I think we all need. Becky tells me she always gets presents just right and spoils the family with her treats and kindness. With a hectic work schedule she had told them that she was too busy to travel from London for the opening, but as she pops her head around the door she smiles and says, "You didn't seriously think I would miss this did you?"

The daily life of the shop soon becomes established and it is not long before Becky has made friends with other traders in the village and together they devise a gift package that combines all their talents. This gift enables the recipient to have her hair done and her make-up professionally applied, she then has her photograph taken and leaves, looking gorgeous, with one of Becky's hand-tied bouquets.

Sweet Peas

Two regular visitors to the shop are Becky's daughters, Amy and Emily, who help their mum make up posies from the 'bits bucket'.

View from the Potting Shed
Steep stone steps, one by one,
Path stretched out in the evening sun.
Splash the birdbath as you pass
Fragrant lines of new cut grass.

Skirt the bed of pinks and stocks,
Aster hobnobs with the phlox.
Slip behind the shimmering hedge,
Enter a world of canes and veg.

Dank green compost, hold your nose,
Tiptoe where the nettle grows.
Grandpa watching from the shed
White socks in the strawberry bed.

Thank you Becky

September

in Buxton

As you approach Buxton from the west you drive through green, craggy valleys with fast flowing rivers, then up onto expansive moors, before you dip down into more intimate, wooded countryside and sweep into the town.

I had forgotten how beautiful the Peak District is. The last time I spent any time in this part of England I was on a geography field trip. Instead of striding out into the hills to record 'terracing' and 'limestone pavements' some of us schoolgirls bought postcards and sketched away in the warmth of a café. This time I am determined to take a closer look.

Green Pavilion

I come across Claire Foster's Green Pavilion Florist and the adjoining Green Pavilion Café by happy accident as I am exploring the Peak District. Turning the corner by the old Spa Baths in Buxton I nearly crash on seeing the abundance of dusky pink and mauve flowers and plants cascading in front of the window of Claire's shop.

Inside, the shop is a riot of bright, autumnal colours vibrant against the many shades of green. It is as if the whole shop is turning with the seasons. Claire and her staff, all dressed in chocolate brown t-shirts, immediately make me feel at home. On a blackboard at the back of the shop is a list of 'Flower Cocktails' – I can tell that I am going to get along with these women.

Flower Cocktails
Martini: Classic bouquet of lilies and foliage.
Cosmopolitan: Stylish sophisticated bouquet for a sophisticated lady (or gent).
Strawberry Daiquiri: A dozen red roses, lusciously wrapped.
B52: A bouquet guaranteed to sweep her off her feet.

I must confess I have a particular fondness for Cosmopolitans. I don't really like rich desserts (much to my girlfriends' disgust) but I can always be persuaded to order a Cosmopolitan instead of a pudding.

Claire and the girls are trying to sort out a number of problems. What should they send to a lady whose errant boyfriend is trying very hard to win her back? Over the past weeks he has sent her bouquets, orchids, roses, and jewellery hidden amongst flowers. The girls think a large, heart-shaped, chocolate cake might do the trick. Claire, who knows the lady in question, thinks she may well be thawing but daren't say anything to her customer yet.

Another problem is what to send to Linda and Debbie, two local beauticians, who are leaving work as they are both expecting babies. As today is their last day there are already sixteen bouquets on order for them from their clients. Claire says they were going to send each of them a 'good luck' bouquet but she now decides to send them a vase each instead.

flower shop secrets
CLAIRE'S SECRET

For a stylish but quick table arrangement put about three inches of water in a goldfish bowl and twist some contorted hazel around the inside of the bowl. Then place chrysanthum blooms, cut very short, in the bottom of the vase.

Another tip for autumn: take a glass vase and then place a smaller vase inside it. Fill the space in between with conkers and then place your flowers in the second vase.

The Green Pavilion Café

Next door to the flower shop is the Green Pavilion Café which is owned by Claire, her husband, Jason (who has a real passion for cooking) and their friend Hannah. When Hannah was younger she visited New Zealand and on her return to Derbyshire she wanted to create food that had the same informal, fresh approach she had experienced on her travels. Consequently the café serves mainly home-made food with the emphasis on interesting, local ingredients. This idea seems to have paid off and the café has recently won a number of food awards.

Many customers shop in both the flower shop and the café. One such customer, an elderly gentleman, Mr Honey, often lunches at the Green Pavilion Café and then calls in next door to buy freesias for the ladies he visits.

On one of my trips to Buxton I am enjoying lunch in the café with my partner, Billy Kelly, when my attention is drawn to a couple at a table in front of the window. They are unpacking books they have just bought at a local book shop. As I love book shops, almost as much as I love flower shops, I decide to try and locate this shop, Scriveners.

Later that afternoon we find ourselves in the best second-hand book shop I have ever seen. Happily speechless we wander absorbed throughout the five floors of books. Billy, who inherited his love of books from his father, has for years been searching for a copy of one of the first books his father introduced him to. Browsing in one of Scrivener's more cramped corners he turns around to be brought face to face with the gilded lettering of this much sort after book, 'The Gathering of Brother Hilarius'.

The Green Pavilion Café tries to source most of its ingredients from within a thirty mile radius of Buxton. On a brisk, changeable day Jason, and Claire's dog, Fozzie (he gets the front seat), drive me up to the next valley to see their egg supplier.

Rushop Edge Farm

Looking out over a broad, undulating valley it is possible to see the clouds sweeping in as the day changes. Although beautiful in the sunshine I can imagine how quickly this turns raw and cold when the weather rolls in.

The family is away at market, but daughter, Susan, introduces us to the hens and ducks that roam around the outside of the farmhouse and on the hillside. She proudly shows us the young calves they have reared which are housed in a nearby barn. Some of the chickens have found their way in here too, perching on the stacks of hay bales.

*"Now and again I like to see
A hen who still runs wild and free,*

*Who cocks her head when roosters crow,
Who knows all things that hens should know."*
Elizabeth Coatsworth

The Pavilion Gardens

Back in Buxton a girl walks into the shop, she is on her mobile phone laughing. She has come in to order a bouquet from her dad to her mum. The message on the card is to say, "Hiya Love, could we go to the caravan early on Saturday morning so I can watch the match? Love you loads."

A teacher from one of the local primary schools calls in to order an arrangement for Mrs Bunting, their recently retired headmistress. They just want her to know they are missing her. Claire tells me that Mrs Bunting was one of her best loved teachers at school and is now one of her favourite customers.

CLAIRE'S FAVOURITES

Flower: *Rose, especially Sweet Avalanche.*

Book: *The Time Traveller's Wife by Audrey Niffenegger.*

Film: *Some Like it Hot.*

Food: *Cheese on toast accompanied by some home-made chutney.*

Drink: *Coffee made on my fantastic, salmon-pink coffee machine, "Gloria".*

Fragrance: *Jo Malone's lime, mandarin & basil perfume.*

View: *The sight of a chilled glass of wine sitting on my kitchen table at the end of a hectic day.*

Animal: *Without doubt my scruffy, wiry terrier Fozzie.*

Record: *Home by Zero 7.*

"You may break, you may shatter the vase, if you will,
But the scent of the roses will hang round it still."
Thomas Moore

Claire and I walk across the park in front of her shop, following the graceful curve of the Georgian crescent around to the Buxton Opera House. Claire is to prepare flowers for a customer who has guests coming for a pre-theatre supper. Her customer, Louise, owns the town's oldest hotel and has been a big supporter of Claire during her years as a florist.

Louise's elegant apartment, which is situated above a pretty teashop, overlooks the Edwardian Opera House and the Pavilion Gardens. As we are working we hear the tinkle of the teashop's doorbell down below. Claire tells me that the flower shop has been buzzing with proud mums buying posies for their talented daughters who are appearing in tonight's opening performance.

A Pre-Theatre Supper

A table arrangement of Claire's favourite Sweet Avalanche roses, mixed with celosia, sedum and hypericum

Mr Foster's Flower Shop

Claire's husband, Jason, is also a florist and runs his own shop in the nearby town of Chapel-en-le-Frith. Claire and Jason met at school when they were both fourteen and became involved with flowers through Jason's family who run a fruit and vegetable business.

There is a lot of laughing rivalry between them and Jason feels it is only fair that I also visit his shop. On first appearance the shop does not look that promising. The outside is obscured by rows of plant trolleys and a crisp, brown, Christmas tree is still hanging from the wall (Jason later tells me that doves have nested there, so he won't move it). But turning the corner into the shop I am spellbound by the beautiful array of flowers. There are rows of blush-coloured orchids peeping out from behind old-fashioned jugs suspended from the low ceiling, there are sumptuous, autumn bouquets and candle-lit displays of rich, red posies. I can quite understand the doves wanting to live here.

Claire and Jason both argue that they cannot work together but as they talk about some of the projects they have collaborated on it is clear that they do make a good team. Claire shakes her head and says, "We say 'yes' and then I wonder, why did we say we could do that?!" But it seems they do find a way to pull it off; whether it is producing a 'wall of orchids' for Singapore Airlines, providing flowers for the Duchess of Devonshire at nearby Chatsworth House, or travelling out to Ireland to prepare wedding flowers.

Thank you Claire

October
in the Lake District

The Flower Shop

Walking through the park into Ambleside I look across the manicured bowling green to the haunting, heather-coloured mountains that rise above the town. On the edge of the park two little girls are racing around waving a flag they found on the putting green. Their harassed father raises his eyebrows at me, "I don't think they've got the hang of this", he comments, "I think they think they're on the moon!"

Alex Brooker's shop is called, very simply, The Flower Shop, and is found on a steep, narrow lane in the centre of the town. Outside the shop, bright against the grey slate of the building, are piles of pumpkins and gourds.

They have just been raided by the local children as they are holding an 'Ugliest Pumpkin Competition' at school. Alex helped them pick all the gnarled, knobbly, angry looking specimens she could find.

flower shop secrets
ALEX'S SECRET

After carving out part of a pumpkin, Alex fills the hole with soaked Oasis. She then uses this as the base for a seasonal display of Calla lilies, protea and peach ilex. Alex explains that this also works well with other fruit and vegetables as their outer skins help to keep the Oasis moist.

The Flower Shop stretches back into an Aladdin's cave of flowers, crowded with many exotic and striking varieties. Alex is preparing some flowers for a regular customer, Edwina, who particularly likes white, oriental lilies mixed with Monstera leaves. Alex says she thinks their simple, sophisticated look suits this very glamorous customer.

A young couple come into the shop to ask about flowers. Alex is especially pleased to greet them as they are customers who moved away to London and she has not seen them for some time. It transpires they are getting married and would like to book The Flower Shop for the wedding.

Clocks & Tricycles

Many of the flower shops I visit sell more than just flowers; Miss Pickering has a fondness for vintage china and Jan Park sells paintings and perfume. But I have never before come across a flower shop that sells clocks and tricycles.

Tucked away at the back of The Flower Shop, behind some burnished oak leaves, is a coral pink tricycle. Alex grins and claims that she couldn't resist it – and it seems other people cannot either. She sells most of her tricycles to grandparents, often before their grandchildren are born.

In mid October I travel to the Lake District with my two daughters to visit Alex. During our stay she suggests that we go on one of her favourite walks through the Langdale Valley; it is a route she traditionally takes with her family each Boxing Day. Alex recommends we start our walk at Chesters, a café overlooking the river at Skelworth Bridge, and then meander along the valley to the village of Elterwater.

The air feels clean and cool and the autumn leaves look iridescent in the clear light. In Elterwater we stop for a drink at the Britannia Inn before returning to Chesters' wood-burning stove and slices of truly luscious, home-made cake.

Chesters, we learn, is named after a much loved English bull terrier who had an eye for anything forbidden. We are told that tales of his antics are legendary, although he is long gone.

Lakes & Leaves

> *"Everything passes and vanishes;*
> *Everything leaves its trace;*
> *And often you see in a footstep*
> *What you could not see in a face."*
> **William Allingham**

The grave of Thomas Rogers who died ascending Helvellyn

Beside Ullswater, in the shadow of the mountains, the small church of Patterdale looks out over the village cricket pitch. As the girls and I explore the area we wander through the churchyard, discovering many beautifully carved headstones. One mossy, weathered inscription reads, 'To the love of my life'.

One of Alex's favourite clients is The Drunken Duck, a family owned inn which has built a reputation for wonderful food and warm hospitality. It is situated about five minutes from Ambleside and has breathtaking views of the surrounding fells. Alex tells me that at the back of the hotel is a small brewery where another of her good customers is situated. It seems that Simon, who works in the brewery, understands what a difference flowers can make and often orders bouquets from The Flower Shop.

Flowers for a Drunken Duck

On a brilliant autumn day I join Alex as she unloads The Drunken Duck's weekly flower order.

The naming of The Drunken Duck
One morning the innkeeper's wife came down to find all her ducks dead in the road. She was saddened by this but being a practical woman decided to pluck and cook them. The ducks, whose drinking water had mistakenly become mixed with beer, soon revived at this rough treatment and waddled back to their yard half naked. It is said that the wife felt so badly about her error that she used local Hawkshead yarn to knit her ducks jumpers and kilts to keep them warm.

The Drunken Duck
How can you tell if a duck's been drinking?
Does he sail on the pond like Titanic sinking?
Do his tales quacker on for an hour or more?
Does he drop all his change on the bar room floor?
Is a wobble in his waddle a sure fire sign?
Does he lead you in dance as he congas in a line?
If he bumps your beer does he take it as a slight?
Do his keen beady eyes look eager for a fight?
Is his beak full of wisdom way beyond his years?
Does he gaze at you fondly with eyes full of tears?
Is he now best friends with the farmyard cat?
Does he wear a lily pad he's mistaken for a hat?
Will he sing you a song with his glass held high?
And tell all the world that he REALLY can fly!

Coming in from a walk we settle by the fire with tea and freshly baked scones, although we have to share the sofa with our new friend, Kipper, the cat.

On a low table in the sitting room there is an arrangement of bronze chrysanthemum blooms and mustard coloured orchids flecked with burgundy.

In the bar Alex places a glass vase of oriental lilies and waxy, brown anthuriums on the counter next to the Champagne bottles. The barman is very welcoming but as the day is so beautiful we decide to take our drinks across the lane to the tables which overlook the fells.

On one of my visits to The Drunken Duck I fall into conversation with a new guest, Kathryn. She is signing her name in the register and laughing as she has just been married and for a moment had forgotten her new surname. Tucked under her arm is a vase of flowers, which I can't help enquiring about. She confesses that she liked her wedding bouquet so much that she has brought it on honeymoon with her.

I gather that Kathryn and her husband have heard some very good accounts of The Drunken Duck and are really looking forward to the food here. They explain that they had considered going abroad for their honeymoon but then decided they would rather eat their way around the north of England instead.

Alex's Favourites

Flower: *Black-eyed chincherinchee.*

Book: *Liz and Claire Cowling's Straight From The Heart series of floristry books.*

Film: *The Power of One.*

Food: *Sunday breakfast or roast lamb.*

Drink: *Fresh coffee.*

Fragrance: *Gardenia.*

View: *The one from my kitchen window.*

Animal: *Our dog, Teddy.*

Record: *No Ordinary Love by Sade.*

Home on the Farm

High above Lake Windermere is the farm where Alex lives with her daughter, Sophie. Sophie often helps her mum in the shop and even has her own, Sophie-sized, Flower Shop uniform to wear. Sophie confides that the best part is when they go out on deliveries, especially when they visit The Langdale Chase Hotel as they are always pleased to see her there. Alex explains that the housekeeper keeps Sophie busy carrying messages to the chambermaids and lets her work the intercom between the various rooms – a great treat.

Alex is also helped with deliveries by a local lady called Margaret. These journeys have become known as Margaret's Mini Adventures, as they are never quite sure what will happen when Margaret is out delivering. Being outgoing and helpful, Margaret has sometimes been delayed when she helps customers arrange their flowers and she has even been known to tidy their houses for them!

Alex's favourite view: the view from her kitchen window

Alex likes to bring natural materials from the farm to the shop to use in her flower displays. Depending on the season, there are berries and leaves, bark and interesting twigs, as well as eggs from the chickens.

Alex's partner, Pip, and his father, Mike, show me around this family farm where they have been keeping cattle and sheep for over thirty years. They are well known locally and can be relied upon to lend a hand in the community when needed. This has included helping to fit the bar at their local pub, The Queen's Head. They tell me this is the only pub that has an antique four-poster bed as a bar!

Thank you Alex

November

in Yarm

Carl Banks

With its wide cobbled streets, Yarm is a pleasant and friendly town about half an hour south of the city of Durham. Carl Banks has run his shop here for over twenty years, even though, as Carl explains, when he took over the old ice cream shop that was on the site, the owner did warn him, "A flower shop? It will never last." Carl was very young when he first started selling flowers. On Thursdays he would play truant from school to visit a flower wholesaler before setting up a market stall in the town. Thursdays stretched into Fridays and his flower business had begun in earnest. Although, he recalls wryly, as he was just a boy he had to rely on his older sister to drive him to the wholesalers.

Carl admits that he gained much of his floristry and business knowledge from a florist who took him under her wing. He recounts how this businesswoman, who had a reputation locally for being rather fierce, showed him great kindness.

Some customers are still remembered from those early days. Carl first met one couple when they travelled by taxi to a weekly dance in Middlesbrough. The taxi driver suggested that Carl went along for the ride and the couple gave him sixpence or a Matchbox car when he jumped out to open the doors for them. Many years later, when the lady was a widow and had lost her sight, Carl would send a box of the first hyacinths of the season to the nursing home where she lived near her family in Kent.

In the cold November sunshine the pavement display is a mixture of luminous greens and whites against a background of woody browns and terracotta. Alison, who started as a Saturday girl here around twelve years ago, brings in an armful of scarlet cyclamens for a customer.

Beside the counter, Ruth, who has very nearly completed twenty years working in the shop, is taking an order from a customer whose daughter is moving house.

Another local lady who helps Carl is retired school teacher, Miss Jessop. With her beautiful handwriting and faultless spelling, Carl asks her to write the card messages out for him when the shop is very busy.

In a hurricane lamp a pile of fresh apples is heaped on a layer of sand. The apples are from the local violin teacher's garden. Carl tells me she is very fond of anemones and is happy to receive these in return for her fruit and hydrangeas.

Old Familiar Faces

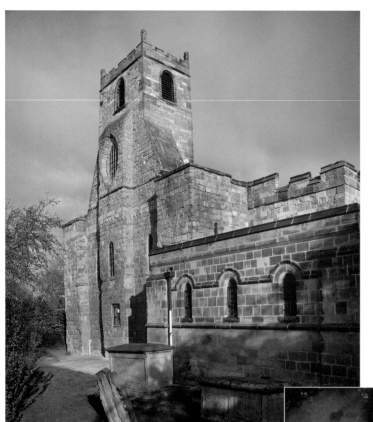

The ladies from the church drop the key into the shop so Carl can prepare flowers for a memorial service. As we enter the church, the sun slants through grey rain clouds lighting up the stained glass windows. Beside the lilies depicted there, is the inscription, 'This is my beloved son in whom I am well pleased'.

*"I look back at it amid the rain
For the last time; for my sand is sinking,
And I shall traverse old love's domain
Never again."*

Thomas Hardy

Carl has seen many families pass through this church. He tells me of one former customer's rather sad and poignant funeral. Few of her family came to the service, but Carl attended, as did the butcher who read the eulogy. As the funeral cortege passed the Town Hall the flag there was lowered to half mast in recognition of her contribution to the community.

"All, all are gone, the old familiar faces."
Charles Lamb

CARL'S FAVOURITES

Flower: *Anemone.*

Book: *Kez by Barry Hines.*

Film: *Beautiful Thing.*

Food: *Roast beef and Yorkshire pudding on a lazy Sunday.*

Drink: *I just like drink!*

Fragrance: *Violets.*

View: *Runswick Bay near Whitby.*

Animal: *Betsy.*

Record: *Carmen.*

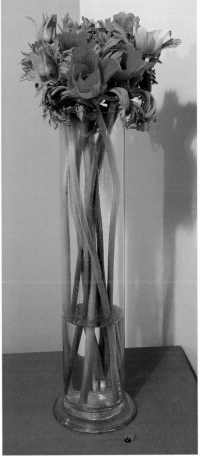

Carl arranges bouquets of monkshood, roses and amaryllis beside a bench in the centre of the shop and carries other posies onto the doorstep. Further up the street he spots 'the girls who lunch' who are window-shopping. These two friends regularly visit the shop and often manage to persuade him to do a deal, with the argument, "My friend would like one too!"

Hidden away at the back of the shop are boxes of foliage and flowers. These have been put aside for a floristry class Carl will be running tomorrow. Beside them are more boxes full of Christmas ribbons and candles that have been brought down from the storeroom ready for the busy month ahead.

My friend, Diane, travels down from her home in Durham to join me for coffee and shopping. It is rare that we get such uninterrupted time together and we spend two glorious hours pottering around the shops for nothing in particular.

I buy a calendar called 'Friends and Flowers' which seems to sum up this whole year's adventure. I know that some people prefer to visit cathedrals and monuments armed with learned guide books – but I have to say this flower shop travel is my idea of heaven.

Dressed for Winter

It is no surprise that many customers ask Carl to prepare wreaths for their doors. What does surprise me though is that some people cannot seem to wait until Christmas to have their doors beautifully decorated and they order their wreaths in November.

We wander down a small side street to deliver some plants and to dress one of the doors there. In the distance the Yarm viaduct towers over the town. This viaduct was built in 1848 and has forty three impressive arches that help carry trains over the River Tees.

Betsy comes with us on our delivery round, cocking her head on one side to consider Carl's handiwork. On the way back to the shop she pops into the green-grocer's as she is certain their will be a welcome and a biscuit for her. Betsy came to the flower shop five years ago and finding she liked it has stayed ever since.

flower shop secrets

CARL'S SECRET

When Carl prepares potted amaryllis and hyacinths for the shop he covers the compost around the plants with moss. When Christmas is approaching he also places ilex or hawthorne berries amongst the moss to give a seasonal twist to the pots.

Amaryllis
What a dress you would make,
Such a rich, soft, sumptuous red.
A dress for candlelight and confidences,
Velvet folds brushing silken legs.
A firelight flick on the floor by a closing door,
Fragrance and memories caught in your ripples.
What a dress you would make.

Thank you Carl

December

in Sussex

Spriggs

With such an appropriate name I cannot resist visiting the Spriggs family as part of my year's journey. The family have been florists in the pretty Sussex town of Petworth for nearly thirty years. As soon as I see their shop and am welcomed by the family and staff, I feel sure this is an excellent way to conclude my months of travelling. A good place to enjoy a last glass of wine and to squeeze in a final bit of shopping.

Working alongside Mr and Mrs Spriggs is their son, Matthew, and their daughter, Samantha. Matthew is now the creative driving force in the business and Samantha who admits to "never touching a flower", is an invaluable support to them all. She explains that she looks after the brides, the quotes, the books and the cuts and bruises.

Before Mr Spriggs senior was a florist he worked as a landscape gardener and he regales me with tales of the many places he has worked. These include twenty-three award-winning gardens at Chelsea and involved helping to restore Kew Palace Gardens after the bombing of the Second World War. And if you visit the shop ask him to tell you about his gardening conversations with the Queen. Gently discrete, Mr Spriggs does not wish me to write about them here, but pop into the shop and you might be able to persuade him to tell you these charming stories.

Petworth is getting dressed for Christmas. Trees are hung up around the streets and the shop windows are a mass of silver, gold and red decorations.

Despite the festive spirit the day-to-day work of the shop continues. There are people to be thanked and congratulated and, sadly, winter funeral pieces to prepare and loved ones to console.

A new delivery of flowers is unpacked; most are displayed in the shop with the remainder being stored in the cellar that runs underneath this old building. The main rooms of the shop are attractively panelled in wood and it is thought that these were constructed by craftsmen, in return for lodgings, when they were employed as carpenters nearby many years ago.

Sue, who has worked for Spriggs for twenty years, enjoys helping customers pick out flowers and she had learnt to recognise what different characters are likely to choose. Whether it is the big, blousy blooms favoured by local artist, Beverley, or the cerise freesias being admired by an elderly gentleman browsing in the shop.

One new customer, who all the staff are convinced is a Russian countess, calls in with her entourage for a magnificent arrangement of lilies.

I gather from Matthew that the foliage they use in their arrangements comes from a number of sources, including the royal estates at Windsor and the private gardens of neighbouring Petworth House. Although, he confesses, they are currently missing John, who is one of their regular foliage suppliers. John is a retired Dutch gentleman who, I am told, has a twinkle in his eye and a weakness for dancing. John has just had a hip operation so delivering the foliage and dancing will have to wait for a while.

In the corner of the shop Samantha's west highland white takes a nap. Samantha found her at the Battersea Dogs' Home and it was only once she had picked her out that Samantha discovered her name was Petal. I wonder if this makes her Petal Spriggs?

Matthew's Garden

Stretching out behind the shop, screened off by a high brick wall, is the garden of Matthew's house. Even in the winter it is a pleasure to explore, with deep magenta and lime-coloured hellebores emerging and spring bulbs just starting to peep through. It is a place Matthew can relax in, and – after seventy weddings already this year – I can understand he would need to escape. He laughs and says, "Before this year I had a full head of hair!"

Underneath the garden table Matthew stores spare branches of pine for the shop, bundles of which will be taken to Petworth House this weekend for a Christmas wreath workshop he is running for The National Trust.

Delivering
to
the
Manor
House

We drive through the wooded Sussex countryside, past red brick farmhouses and villages to deliver flowers to one of Matthew's customers. We are to decorate their fireplaces and doors with garlands and wreaths in preparation for a family Christmas.

"The snow is lying very deep.
My house is sheltered from the blast.
I hear each muffled step outside,
I hear each voice go past."
Agnes Lee

In the warm kitchen the scents of oranges, cloves and cinnamon mixes with the fresh fragrance of the pine. I would really like to pour myself a large glass of red wine and toast my feet by the fire but I am not sure the owners of the house would appreciate it!

Christmas Shopping in Petworth

My friend, Jennifer, who works with me at Ted Martin Flowers, joins me in Petworth for some Christmas shopping. She is enchanted by Spriggs and I soon find Matthew and Jennifer deep in conversation. We then spend an agreeable few hours exploring Petworth, making sure we call into all the shops that Spriggs has helped decorate for the Christmas season.

We take up Samantha's suggestion and stop at The Angel for a couple of glasses of red wine by the fire. This is so enjoyable and cosy that wine turns into lunch, at the end of which Jennifer has befriended the new owners and we are given a guided tour of the refurbished bedrooms. And very nice they are too.

Heavenly Drawers

How much is that doggy in the window?

233

The Christmas House Party

I join Matthew and his team as they help to decorate Hollycombe House for a weekend of Christmas celebrations. There is to be a shooting party and a number of guests are invited to dinner. A large carol concert is also to take place on the lawn in front of the house. As I arrive preparations are well underway and there is a busy and jolly atmosphere.

The ladders have just been removed from the front porch where columns have been adorned with pine swags and berries. Spriggs' florist, Ellen, emerges carrying a large door wreath – dodging the butler who is starting to unload a huge pile of logs for the fires.

I follow Ellen back into the house and chat to her as she finishes creating a stunning display of hydrangeas and amaryllis. We both agree this is a beautiful house and Ellen says coming here makes her want to go home and rearrange her own house. I laugh and tell her it makes me want to go home and move house!

We are made very welcome by Matthew's customer, Virginia, and when I compliment her on her wonderful house she says simply, "It's our home." And it does feel like it is a very warm and friendly home.

Looking out over the darkening parkland, Virginia's study desk is piled with Christmas packages and parcels. Tucked into the mirror by the clock on the mantelpiece is a jumble of Christmas invitations and cards.

Spriggs' florist, Darren, helps to arrange a large garland around the huge fireplace in the hall. He tells me that later on they will hang pine swagging from the balustrade around the landing. As the whole team is getting into the Christmas spirit he says most of them decided to wear red today.

A wreath full of berries, cones and feathers

I watch Samantha as she prepares a large trough of orchids for a side table. I quiz her about this as I have heard her claim that she never touches flowers. She grins and says, it is always such fun here at Christmas that she didn't want to be left out.

The fires are lit and Virginia organises a tray of tea for the florists.

In the dining room a large garland of decorated pine is snaked along the centre of the table in between the candelabras and the frosted nightlights. The silver and glassware are polished and set ready. It is all starting to look very festive.

In the drawing room Matthew has decided to keep the colour scheme to frosted silver and white. This enables him to use his favourite flower, white amaryllis.

MATTHEW'S FAVOURITES

Flower: *White amaryllis.*

Book: *The Pursuit of Love by Nancy Mitford.*

Film: *Star Trek, First Contact.*

Food: *Duck, in any way, shape or form, especially oriental.*

Drink: *Mimosa Champagne Cocktail (Champagne, Cointreau and orange juice).*

Fragrance: *Jo Malone grapefruit-scented candle.*

View: *The lake in Petworth Park on a frosty morning with the mist hanging over the water.*

Animal: *Clara, my daschund, of course.*

Record: *Forever Autumn by Justin Hayward.*

flower shop secrets
MATTHEW'S SECRET

The bottoms of Amaryllis stems often split and curl up making it difficult to fit them into the bottom of the vase. Matthew suggests slipping a rubber band around the end of each stem to stop this happening.

A job well done. And now it is time for a Spriggs' family Christmas.

Master Spriggs, Clara Spriggs, Mrs Spriggs, Miss Spriggs and Mr Spriggs

The Last Chapter

There is one last journey to make. Having met all these talented and hard working florists from the length and breadth of England I thought it was only right to bring them all together so they could meet each other. It seemed to me that they would have an exceptional amount in common and have much to discuss and share. And I was certain it would be a great opportunity for furthering friendships and having fun.

So, on a wintry day with rain threatening, the florists travel from all over the country to meet in the Cotswolds. Despite the prospect of some long journeys everyone is very enthusiastic about getting together. We gather at The Bay Tree Hotel in Burford, where the fires are lit and the Champagne is waiting. I ask Ted and Jennifer to come and join us too as I feel they are also part of my flower shop journey – and they have had to listen to my stories all year!

Some of us decide to make a weekend of it and book rooms at The Bay Tree Hotel, where the staff could not make us feel more welcome and looked after. Becky arrives from Lincolnshire with a bouquet for me, whilst Nicki, from Henley on Thames, brings me a jar of fragrant hyacinths tied with a black and white spotty ribbon. I insist on having these in my room so I can enjoy them to their full.

It is so lovely to see everyone together – and I was right, it is great fun. Marcelle and Becky get chatting and having spotted a flower shop in Burford, Eden Flowers, they go off together to explore. The shop is shut but they manage to peer in the window at the soft pastel roses there. Another flower shop to be explored at a later date ...

Sipping a glass of Champagne in front of the fire I reflect on my year. I have travelled thousands of miles, I have visited parts of England I didn't really know and discovered new things about the places I thought I knew. I have made good friends and I feel enormously privileged to have been allowed a glimpse of their worlds. I could say that there have been times when it has been tiring and very hard work but it would be closer to the truth to say that my year has been a complete joy.

"Life is partly what we make it and partly what is made by the friends we choose."
Tennessee Williams

Matthew
Spriggs
December

Rachel
Rachel Lilley
April

Simon & Marcelle
Smith Street Deli
July

Carl
Carl Banks
November

Alex
The Flower Shop
October

Jason & Claire
Green Pavilion
September

Keith & Marc
Vaas
February

Nicki
White Gdn
June

Miss Pickering
Miss Pickering
March

Jan
blue
May

Becky
Potting Shed Florist
August

Leen
the flower boutique
January

Sally Page

January

the flower boutique,
61a High Street, Linton,
Cambridgeshire, CB21 4HS,
01223 891740
info@theflowerboutiquelinton.co.uk
www.theflowerboutiquelinton.co.uk

The Stables,
Spains Hall, Finchingfield, Essex,
CM7 4NJ,
01371 811256
www.spainshall.co.uk

Alimentum,
152-154 Hills Road, Cambridge,
CB2 8PB
01223 413000
www.restaurantalimentum.co.uk

February

VAAS,
20 - 22 Heathcoat Street, Hockley,
Nottingham, NG1 3AA,
0115 959 8959
post@vaas.co.uk   www.vaas.co.uk

Harts Hotel,
Standard Hill, Park Row,
Nottingham, NG1 6GN,
0115 988 1900
www.hartsnottingham.co.uk

March

Miss Pickering,
7 St.Paul's Street, Stamford,
Lincolnshire, PE9 2BE,
01780 482961
flowers@misspickering.com
www.misspickering.com

George Hotel,
71 St Martins, Stamford,
Lincolnshire, PE9 2LB,
01780 750750
www.georgehotelofstamford.co.uk

Contact details

**The Olive Branch
& Beech House
Village Inn**,
Main Street, Clipsham, Rutland,
LE15 7SH,
01780 410355
www.theolivebranchpub.com

Jennifer Bell (Artist),
153 Musters Road, West Bridgford,
Nottingham, NG2 7AF,
0115 9817306
www.campionbell.com

Naylor Flowers,
The Old Pack House,
Moulton Common,
Spalding,
Lincolnshire,
PE12 6LF,
01205 260649
www.naylorflowers.co.uk

April

Rachel Lilley,
13 London Street,
Bath, BA1 5BU,
01225 319485
rachel@rachellilley.com
www.rachellilley.com

The Bertinet Kitchen,
12 St Andrew's Terrace, Bath,
01225 445531
www.thebertinetkitchen.com

Dyrham Park,
nr Bath, Gloucestershire,
SN14 8ER,
0117 937 2501
www.nationaltrust.org.uk

May

blue,
11 Victoria Road, Shifnal,
Shropshire, TF11 8AF,
01952 462626
jan@blue-shifnal.co.uk
www.blue-shifnal.co.uk
also at:
23 Wyle Cop,
Shrewsbury, SY1 1XB,
01743 366200

David Austin Roses,
Bowling Green Lane,
Albrighton, Wolverhampton,
WV7 3HB,
01902 376301
www.davidaustinroses.com

June

White Gdn,
19a Hart Street,
Henley-on-Thames,
Oxfordshire, RG9 2AR,
01491 577370
info@white-gdn.co.uk
www.white-gdn.co.uk

Barn Galleries,
Middle Culham Farm, Aston,
Henley-on-Thames,
Oxfordshire, RG9 3DX,
01491 577786
www.barngalleries.com

Floyd Shoes,
Old Vineyards Farmhouse,
Charlton Hill, Cheltenham,
GL53 9NE,
01242 529920
www.floydshoes.co.uk

La Campana,
20 Bell Street,
Henley-on-Thames,
Oxon,
RG9 2AR
01491 573412